Pope Joan: The Indestructible Legend of the Catholic Church's First and Only Female Pontiff

By Charles River Editors

A 16th century manuscript depicting Pope Joan with the papal tiara

About Charles River Editors

Charles River Editors is a boutique digital publishing company, specializing in bringing history back to life with educational and engaging books on a wide range of topics. Keep up to date with our new and free offerings with this 5 second sign up on our weekly mailing list, and visit Our Kindle Author Page to see other recently published Kindle titles.

We make these books for you and always want to know our readers' opinions, so we encourage you to leave reviews and look forward to publishing new and exciting titles each week.

Introduction

A 15ᵗʰ century depiction of Pope Joan

Pope Joan

"I do not wish women to have power over men; but over themselves." – Mary Shelley

The Middle Ages in Europe were some of the most precarious centuries in recorded history, bristling with war, excitement, and chaos. The Western Roman Empire had crumbled, territories were rapidly expanding, and heavy ploughs, hourglasses, spectacles, tidal mills, and more pioneering inventions were popping up across the continent. It was also a time of extreme prejudice, when women were treated as second-class citizens. Their only purpose in life was to procreate by the dozen. They were confined to their kitchens and barns at home. They could not vote, and most definitely were not allowed to be involved in anything with the word "office" in its title. What was worse, only a handful of these women would succeed in hauling themselves out of the trenches, as females were not allowed an education.

Given this context, there have always been stories about women who broke the mold somehow, and of all the mysterious stories passed down over the centuries and chronicled by history's storytellers, one of the most fascinating and hotly contested subjects is Pope Joan, a young woman who was so desperate to squeeze herself out of the status quo that she had done the unthinkable. For decades, she disguised herself as a man, living amongst her oppressors as she paved her way to the papal throne. She would keep up this pretense for more than 2 years until that one fateful day, when it all came unraveling.

By the early 13th century, the tale of a female pope who presided over the Catholic Church a few centuries earlier was making its way across Europe. In fact, in *Chronica Universalis Mettensis*, Jean de Mailly fleshed out a number of details: "Query: Concerning a certain Pope or rather female Pope, who is not set down in the list of popes or Bishops of Rome, because she was a woman who disguised herself as a man and became, by her character and talents, a curial secretary, then a Cardinal and finally Pope. One day, while mounting a horse, she gave birth to a child. Immediately, by Roman justice, she was bound by the feet to a horse's tail and dragged and stoned by the people for half a league, and, where she died, there she was buried, and at the place is written: 'Petre, Pater Patrum, Papisse Prodito Partum' [Oh Peter, Father of Fathers, Betray the childbearing of the woman Pope]. At the same time, the four-day fast called the 'fast of the female Pope' was first established."

As others took it up and spread it along, the legend of Pope Joan became a gripping tale of bravery and treachery, replete with drama, complete with a mystery lover, surprising twists, and even a cliffhanger. But of course, the overhanging question is whether Pope Joan really existed. Many, including modern historians and the Roman Catholic Church, are quick to dismiss Joan's story as myth, but others beg to differ and believe in the actual historical existence of a woman who would inevitably be one of the Church's most groundbreaking popes.

Pope Joan: The Indestructible Legend of the Catholic Church's First and Only Female Pontiff looks at the riveting story of Pope Joan, including an examination of all the various theories regarding the legend's veracity. Along with pictures depicting important people, places, and events, you will learn about Pope Joan like never before.

The Context for Joan's Story

"But I would have you know, that the head of every man is Christ; and the head of the woman is the man; and the head of Christ is God." – 1 Corinthians 11:3

They say truth is often stranger than fiction, and a dive into the annals of history provides countless stories awash with awful accidents, curious coincidences, and mystifying mysteries. There was the tragic 1986 Chernobyl disaster, the worst and most expensive nuclear accident in all of history, with damages totaling $200 billion, conservatively. Another well-known accident would be the sinking of the Titanic, which claimed the lives of 1,503 people after colliding with an iceberg. In the book of real-life creepy coincidences, there is the case surrounding celebrated horror writer Edgar Allan Poe, who wrote "The Narrative of Arthur Gordon Pym of Nantucket." The short story tells the tale of 3 whalers stranded at sea who cannibalize their cabin boy, Richard Parker. In 1846, 8 years after the novel was published, a man named Richard Parker perished along with 20 others in a boating accident. Even stranger, 46 years after the story hit the stands, a 17-year-old cabin boy fell into a coma, and his body was feasted on by the remaining 3 crewmen. Most chilling of all, the boy's name just happened to be Richard Parker.

The most persistent and multifaceted are the jewels of history's mysteries. Some of the most fascinating unresolved mysteries include the still-debated identities behind notorious murderers, such as Jack the Ripper or the Zodiac Killer. Plot twists have been and continue to be found in not only every corner of history, but in recent events. There is the classic story of the Trojan Horse, a giant wooden horse packed with Greek warriors that snuck into the city of Troy, killing its unsuspecting army and ending the war.

Among the most awe-inspiring plot twists to ever surface are history's greatest pretenders. These were the masqueraders whose disguises fooled not only the public, but those around them for so long, that their real identities were only unveiled at the time of their deaths. There was the intoxicating Mata Hari, an exotic dancer and courtesan who was executed for moonlighting as a spy during World War I. A more morbid example comes in the form of Gilles de Rais, who had fought alongside Joan of Arc, his reputation later irreparably damaged when he confessed to the multiple killings of innocent children.

Peppered into these stories of history's greatest and most stunning impostors are those that took it one step further by reversing typical gender roles. One of the most widely-circulated accounts is the story of Shi Pei Pu, an opera singer from Beijing turned spy. Not only had he managed to convince a French government worker that he was a woman to collect secrets for his side, their sexual relationship was one that lasted 2 decades.

In fact, breaking down the traditional gender roles set by society's norms has been one of the tallest and rockiest of the mountains in humanity's seemingly endless range of challenges. Even today, in various parts of the world, women and young girls of all ages still face an excruciatingly long road ahead to gender equality. With that in mind, a series of brave women – many of them nameless and their stories unheard – have ventured forth to break the stereotypes, wreaking havoc in a world often dominated by men.

Some 200,000 years ago, people began to make their homes across the then wet and fertile terrains of Africa, and as civilization began to unfurl, gender roles were created to determine the division of labor. Men, as the more physically robust of the sexes, built shelters, tools, and took on hunting, whereas women stayed home, foraged, and looked after the babies. While the hunter-gatherer tribes may be of common knowledge, anthropological evidence hints at an egalitarian society where both men and women lived in peace, and were treated equally. They even embraced ideas still regarded as highly liberal in today's societies, including polygamy and promiscuity.

In the millennia that followed, the growing population of humans began to spread across the globe. Slowly but surely, different cultures and norms evolved within these budding societies. In the same pace, a new trend of patriarchal societies emerged, one that still lives on in certain cultures of the modern age.

The first patriarchy emerged in the Neolithic Era, roughly 8,000 to 12,000 years ago. Egalitarian societies started to unravel, and the idea of private ownership began to appeal to the masses. The men of these communities began to see themselves as the head of their families, and in many societies, women were minimized to inferior reproductive machines and caretakers. In an age way before pregnancy tests, women were forced to stay virgins until marriage so that men would know that their offspring belonged to them.

In other villages, women were seen as property. Arranged marriages were common, conducted by fathers with no input from the daughters, who were up for bid. Some tribal chiefs were said to have offered virgins and young women as a welcoming courtesy to foreign visitors. Worse yet, rape frenzies were aplenty in certain village festivals, sanctioned by their leaders as a way to "promote prosperity."

On the other side of the world, in the polis system of Ancient Greece, which is considered the earliest example of a democracy, all men were awarded equal rights. Women, on the other hand, saw theirs snatched away from them. Women had no other alternative but to be wives and mothers, as dictated by law, and those who refused were punished. Married women saw no more rights than single women – they could not inherit property or leave the house without permission, had no legal custody of their offspring, and were killed when found guilty of the crime of adultery.

Naturally, gender roles varied from culture to culture. In ancient China, the patriarchy formed the crux of most societies, which were largely molded by Confucian philosophy. Though one of China's most powerful leaders, Empress Wu ZeTian of the Tang Dynasty, was a woman, females were far from counterparts. This is especially highlighted in the well-documented years of female infanticide that would plague that nation for over 2,000 years.

Confucian teachings placed women at the bottom of the hierarchy. The Chinese character for the word "woman" itself is said to depict a woman kneeling, signifying obedience. Husbands were under "duty" to remarry, but a woman was never to be a bride again. During the early years of the Qing dynasty, childbearing was so crucial that childless widows were known to commit suicide over the shame of being unable to produce. Beauty standards were established, including the now-extinct tradition of foot-binding. Concubinage, which was also prevalent in cultures such as Judaism and Islam, were part of everyday life.

In the spirit of filial piety, the only women who were respected were the elders of the village. Villagers often sought out these wise men and women for advice. These older members of society were not only equipped with valuable knowledge built from years of experience, some were believed to have achieved the highest form of enlightenment, and therefore, possessed special "gifts." Other than taking part in an elder community, widows could also boost their ranks. Only by becoming the eldest member of the family was the woman allowed to "wear the pants."

As history progressed, women occasionally wore the crowns, such as the female pharaohs of Ancient Egypt and the monarchs of Europe, but these societies were still very much operated as a patriarchy. Women all over the world were continuously treated as second-class citizens, with the mere idea of holding down an equal-paying job – or any job at all – either downright foreign or laughably unthinkable. To the surprise of few, women began to go far and beyond to break the tradition of oppression. To these women, the only feasible option to get ahead in the patriarchy was to disguise themselves as their oppressors – and this was exactly what they did.

Perhaps the most popular of these stories is captured in the 1998 Disney animation, Mulan. The cartoon was inspired by the ancient Chinese poem, "The Ballad of Mulan," which was about a woman who was said to have lived during the Northern Wei Dynasty. Hua Mulan, a young maiden who was well-versed with weapons and mixed martial arts, disguised herself as a man and enlisted in her father's place during the war, as he was too old and feeble to fight.

Then there's the story of Saint Marina. Marina was another young woman who took up cross-dressing so that she could join a local monastery with her father. There, she became a monk, naming herself Marinus, and lived under this identity for several years. An innkeeper's daughter would later accuse her of fathering her child, but rather than reveal herself, "Marinus" raised the child in the monastery before they were banished from the premises.

In later centuries, more cases featuring similar plot twists seemed to pile on. For years, the Brontë sisters, a talented trio of 19th century writers, published their masterpieces under the shared male pseudonym of "Currer Bell." When asked why, the sisters explained that women writers were "liable to be looked on with prejudice."

Of course, much of Pope Joan's story takes place in Rome, and ancient Rome is often glamorized as a glittering era of culture, innovation, and nonstop action. What's not to love about grand coliseums, classic stone bridges, towering walls of aqueducts, upon other forms of brilliant Roman architecture. Fierce gladiators gliding across the dirt path on glinting chariots, dust flying behind the blurs of the horse's hooves? Not to mention the glorious parties starring extravagant feasts, drunken Romans, and wild orgies into the wee hours of the night, sometimes for weeks on end.

The dark truth of the sometimes ugly reality of life in Ancient Rome is almost never showcased in Hollywood and media. The Ancient Romans have undoubtedly contributed to much of Western civilization thanks to things like the Roman numeral system, papyrus newspapers, and more, but as soon as those Hollywood filters are removed, one would find a life that was far less glamorous. For starters, many Ancient Roman practices could be considered rather barbaric. This was a time when their idea of the Super Bowl was to flock to the arenas to watch criminals get ripped apart by blood-thirsty beasts, all the while placing bets on which bait would be the first to meet their end. Gladiator fights were a beloved sport, which involved a pair of well-trained warriors facing off, wielding spears and tridents. In some cases, the wealthy were allowed to pay extra to witness a fight to the death.

It was only with the nation's transition to Christianity in the 4th century that more of the public began to denounce these sports. By the next century, these arena mega-shows were banned. Some sources put that date to the first of January, in the year 404. It is said that an appalled monk, now Saint Telemachus, stormed into the battlefield in the middle of a gladiator game to put an end to the fight. Sadly, the crowd turned on him and began pelting him with rocks and large objects, stoning him to death. Emperor Honorius was apparently so shaken by the death of the monk that he called for a stop to these games once and for all.

A bust of Honorious

The brutality behind these sports is just one dimension when it came to the everyday lives of the Romans. There was also the nearly non-existent hygiene of the time. Despite pioneering the plumbing system, public toilets were known to explode on the regular from methane build-up. Romans were expected to wipe off with a filthy communal sponge, and urine was used as mouthwash and laundry detergent. Bathing was not common practice, either; instead, Romans coated themselves with perfumed oils, scraped off their dead skin, and called it a day.

Medicinal practices were revolting. Some athletes were known to chug energy drinks blended with goat excrement. Some epileptics topped off vials of gladiator blood after seizures. The sweat and dead skin scrapings of these warriors were even bottled up in face creams and put on the market, attracting queues of wealthy women. Diseases swept across the land, with civilians falling like flies from illness and bad hygiene.

Above all, the least appealing factor was society's abhorrent treatment of its women. As Rome entered the 9th century, Catholicism had become Rome's official religion. Biblical views, which were taken to a drastically literal level those days, formed the foundations of Roman law. As an appetizer, the Church held women accountable for "original sin." Since it was Eve who had taken a bite out of the forbidden fruit during the alleged creation of mankind, the Church decided that the following generations of women would be made to pay for it.

It appears that the bias against women was always been prevalent in Ancient Europe. Even Aristotle, who is still revered by many today as one of the greatest thinkers to have ever lived, held these antiquated beliefs. He insisted that women were "infertile males," deficient for their inability to produce "true" sperm. This, he argued, was why men were above women, otherwise known as "barbarians" in the natural hierarchy, and thus destined to rule over the opposite gender.

A bust of Aristotle

The fact that women seemed almost akin to the evils and demons in the Holy Book itself certainly did not help their case. The Book of Corinthians makes the male's destined supremacy over women abundantly clear. 1 Corinthians 11: 8-9 blatantly states, "For the man is not of the woman, but the woman of the man. Neither was the man created for the woman; but the woman for the man." A later chapter of the same book orders men to control their women: "Let your women keep silence in the churches: for it is not permitted unto them to speak; but they are commanded to be under obedience, as also saith the law." The same sentiments are echoed in other books of the Bible, including the Books of 1st Peter and Timothy.

Women were not only expected to be submissive to their husbands, they were made to dress "moderately." They could only accessorize with 1 to 2 pieces of jewelry, and were prohibited from wearing any flashy garments that could invite attention. Wives had no choice but to be faithful to their husbands if they wanted to avoid being stoned or burnt to death for the crime of being a "whore," according to the Book of Leviticus. Men, however, could have as many concubines as they pleased.

A story in the Book of Judges even tells of a godly man who was so mortified by a drunken mob's wish to sexually assault a man that he offered his virgin daughter to them instead. The man declared, "Do with them [his daughter and a present concubine] what seemeth good unto you; but unto this man do not so vile a thing."

Though the men could not seem to stop themselves from procreating with them, women were branded as mysterious and unnatural creatures. This could be blamed on either the era's primitive knowledge of science and the female anatomy. Or, once again, this paranoia could be attributed to the teachings of the Holy Book.

One of the most celebrated Roman authors, Pliny the Elder, believed that women turned into witches during their cycles. Approximately once a month, a menstruating woman could stop and start hailstorms and natural disasters, kill crops and small creatures, dim mirrors, and blunt the tips of mighty weapons in the blink of an eye. The Book of Leviticus instructed men to stay away from women during their cycles, too, as she would be "ceremonially unclean for 7 days." If a man did not want to be infected by "menstrual impurity," he had to refrain from touching the woman, and could not allow her anywhere near his bed, clothes, or genitals.

Even the very act women were thought to only be good for was held against them. Childbirth was another way a woman was dubbed "unclean," and bearing baby girls called for an extra penalty. Mothers who gave birth to sons were impure for a week, and would be made to stay away from her family for a period of no more than 7 days. Mothers who bore a "maid child" would be unclean for an extra week, and were tasked with re-purifying their blood for a lengthy stretch of 66 days.

Needless to say, official Roman law in the 9th century did not take too kindly to women. In Roman family law, much like the constitutions around the world, men were made the masters of the house. Women belonged to their husbands, and could be punished any way their husbands saw fit. They were never to own property of their own, not even the dowry. Authorities decided that not one woman was equipped with the capacity of making sound judgments and decisions. To them, women were only slightly above, if not equal to the "vermin" of society, which included minorities, the disabled, slaves, and common criminals. And so, women were not allowed to take up a job in public office, vote, fight in the military, represent themselves in court, or sign any legal documents on their own.

In essence, it would be nearly impossible, and obviously undesirable, to imagine spending 24 hours in the shoes of a woman in 9th century Rome. And while these women could do nothing but deal the cards handed to them with a brave face, plenty of them must have reached a breaking point. It was in this suffocating climate of rampant inequality and oppression that an icon would soon be born, with a name so immortal it continues to be mentioned over 1,200 years later.

The Birth of a Rebel

"When a woman has scholarly inclinations, there is usually something wrong with her sexuality." – Friedrich Nietzsche, *Beyond Good and Evil*

Comprehensive records, valuable literature, and historical artifacts juggled by the hands of time can either weather a good beating or slip through the cracks, and the story of Joan is no different. Hers is a story that has been regurgitated by noted historians across Europe over the centuries, and as a result, significant chunks of the story have been lost and details have been altered on numerous occasions. With that said, the following accounts have been woven together through information gathered from various sources, and certain areas have been tweaked but tailored to achieve historical accuracy.

Details of this legendary story have become so hazy that the mere name and birthplace of history's only female pope is unknown. A Dominican chronicler, Jean de Mailly, is credited with one of the story's earliest appearances in the early 13th century, and his version describes an unnamed woman who would rise to the papal throne. One version named their protagonist "Giliberta,", or "Giovanna," and in another, "Agnes."

The version that would eventually stick was the most fleshed out and widely accepted of all these tidbits, and it was authored by Martin Polonus of Opava, a 13th century friar and alleged close advisor to the pope. It was with Martin's version that this character was finally given a name that would be embraced by all.

In the year 815, a pair of English missionaries based in the city of Mainz, Germany, gave birth to a healthy baby girl. As the infant's cries pierced the still of the night, her mother cradled her, rocking in her arms to calm her. The new parents hovered over their child, marveling at their creation, and it was at this moment that they gave her a name. They called her Johanna – or simply, Joan.

Though Joan's parents might have wished for a baby boy, watching their child grow up was a blessing on its own. The infant mortality rates were as high as it had ever been; historians estimated that up to a quarter of all babies born in the Middle Ages never made it past their first year.

Famous figures, real or fictitious, are often attached to distinctive physical traits. Goldilocks has her staple gilded curls. Cleopatra is often depicted with her trademark smoky eyes and dramatic winged tips, lined with black kohl. As for Joan, her appearance, likes, and dislikes could only be left to the imaginations of future generations. In the eyes of painters and sculptors, Joan was a pale, fair-haired woman with a broad forehead and flaxen eyebrows to match. Her wide eyes were deep and soulful, and she had a tall, pointed nose, a trait often associated with wisdom.

Joan's missionary parents were anything but nobility, and lived the simple lives of peasant folk. Like most European peasants of the time, Joan's family would have owned a humble barn, a few animals, and a small plot of land to farm with. At this time, formal education was only available to young boys whose families could afford it, and so, Joan was expected to hang onto the hems of her mother's wispy tunic as she tackled the chores for the day.

Women and young girls not only handled all of the cooking, cleaning, and housework, they were to help the men out on the field. Particularly in the summer, women and their daughters shook each other awake as early as 3 in the morning. A few hours shy of sunrise, Joan and her mother would put on their tunics, bundle up their hair behind their wimples, and head to the kitchen to start breakfast. There, they put together a pottage, or a type of thick, but spice-less stew, with corn, barley, vegetables – and if they were lucky, bits of meat.

After breakfast, Joan and her mother would divvy up their chores. One stayed behind to make more pottage for later meals of the day. When there was enough flour, hard bread could be baked in the communal oven in the village. By the break of dawn, the other exited the mud hut and joined the men in the field. Here, the woman helped weed the fields, fed the small farm animals, and collected berries, herbs, vegetables, and other crops. As many hands as possible were needed on the fields – a bad harvest could mean no food for the frigid winter.

Dusk marked the end of the work day, with an extra working hour or 2 during the summer. After dinner, Joan and her mother would cross off the rest of the chores. They scrubbed the floors and furniture clean. New clothes were woven, spun, and stitched together, and clothes mended. Meats and fish were pickled in jars of salt brine and vinegar, or smoked for longevity. Fruit, meats, and grains were dried out and candied, and honey stirred into barrels of mead. By the end of the day, their hands and feet were riddled with callouses.

Most women had their entire lives spelled out for them. With the average life span at the time set between 30 to 40 years, and most females at 25, some women had become mothers by the age of 13 or 14. But even at an early age, young Joan loathed the monotony of routine women were made to resign themselves to. This was not a life she wanted to pursue, and she was going to make sure of it.

Joan was said to have been a gifted child prodigy, with an unmatched specialty for language. In a time when women and young girls who wandered out into the streets without permission were labeled "prostitutes," Joan, like many other girls, stayed in, and put her time to good use. As soon as she had finished her chores, she would sneak out to the libraries, sometimes staying out and keeping herself preoccupied into the late hours of the night, candle in hand. The young girl soon developed an unbridled obsession for knowledge, and by the time she had become a teenager, she had already mastered German, Latin, and Greek. According to Polonus, Joan would also acquire and become "proficient in a diversity of branches of knowledge."

While other women worked hard to maintain their identities in the confinements of their homes, Joan knew that her potential would be squandered if she restricted herself to a life of domestic submission. Just a few miles away from home lay the Benedictine Fulda Monastery, gorgeous stone towers capped with gray onion-dome roofs. This monastery, which had been in operation since March 12, 744, had earned a reputation as one of the top schools and learning centers in all of Germany.

The school boasted a magnificent *scriptorium*, where monastic scribes sat behind special wooden desks with elevated tabletops. Here, they spent hours writing, copying, and "illuminating" manuscripts, which were essentially handmade books. The monks-in-training also had access to an enormous library that held over 2,000 manuscripts. This was a true haven for German and European literature, which included the rare and prized works of Tacitus, a former senator and historian of the Roman Empire.

It was Joan's dream to be enrolled in the Fulda monastery, but she had no delusions about it. If she were to stroll up and knock on the doors of the monastery, whoever was in charge would take one look at her and promptly slam the door in her face. As much as Joan wanted it, this was an impossible dream Joan knew she would soon have to put to sleep.

Or, maybe not.

Forbidden Love & Broken Vows

"The course of true love never did run smooth." – William Shakespeare, "A Midsummer Night's Dream"

Monks, especially in the Middle Ages, lived anything but a thrilling life. These were men who had willingly chosen to renounce all their material possessions to live a life of godliness and discipline. Forgoing all worldly belongings must have been the easiest part of the process.

Upon entering the monastery, these men essentially signed their lives off to God, vowing to adhere to a life of poverty, chastity, and obedience. For a sense of complete humility and uniformity, Benedictine monks wore heavy habits, with large, loose hoods attached called "cowls." The habits came in limited shades of blotchy white or gray, the color of natural, untreated wool. It would only be a century or 2 later that the Benedictine order began to don ink-black robes, thenceforth known as the "Black Monks." Under those cowls, monks sported "tonsures." These were less than flattering bald spots intentionally shaved off on the top of their heads, the ring of their remaining hair forming a crown of sorts.

A depiction of Saint Benedict of Nursia

A depiction of Benedict of Aniane

The monastery life was defined by routine. Their days consisted of constant prayer, text translation, poring through page after page of the Bible, and self-meditation. The rest of their day was spent crossing off their chore lists, which included cooking, tidying up around the monastery, and other humdrum tasks.

The monastery was designed to fulfill all of its inhabitants' basic needs. Most were outfitted with a school, a clinic, and barber services, so there was never a need for any of the monks to leave their home. Those who left the abbey without permission could be written up for violating the vows of obedience and poverty, but this was a rare case.

The vow of chastity was a whole different ballgame. Monks vowed to remain single and abstinent for life, as they considered themselves married to the Church. Masturbating monks were seen as committing another sin in itself. The Anglo-Saxon *Paenitentiale Theodori,* or the *Canons of Theodore,* which was first published around the beginning of the 8th century, makes this clear: "If he defiles himself, he is to abstain from meat for 4 days...If he is a boy and he does it often, either he is to fast 20 days, or one is to whip him..."

Now, some might scratch their heads and ask themselves why Joan would ever want to take part in such a thing, but it must be remembered that monastic schools were the most prestigious institutions for higher learning during this time period. Sure, she could risk being the talk of the town's gossip committee and become a nun or a hermitess, but unlike most women of the time, Joan valued her education over her religion. Apart from religious studies, monastic schools were at the forefront of science such as astronomy and medicine.

For years, Joan could only yearn from afar, but that was all about to change. One day, as 12-year-old Joan ambled past the Fulda Monastery on her way home, she heard a whisper. Joan spun around, her eyes darting back and forth and her arms prickling with goosebumps. When her roaming eyes finally settled on the face peering back at her from behind a tree trunk, she breathed a sigh of relief. The kind face belonged to a young Benedictine monk. Again, the name and age of this monk has never been verified, with varying sources estimating their age gap to be anywhere from a few years to several decades.

A tentative Joan, who had never before made contact with anyone outside of her family, began to approach him gingerly. The pair struck up a conversation, and when she let her guard down, they became fast friends. They matched up their schedules and committed to a series of secret appointments. For the next couple of weeks, the pair slunk out of their quarters religiously and gathered at their private meeting point.

The monk would fish out the manuscripts he had borrowed from the library. He became her personal tutor, guiding her through the texts and teachings of scholars from a broad collection of sciences. Some lessons covered the 53 mathematical word problems from Alcuin's *Propositiones*. Some covered the teachings from the Hippocratic school of medicine and Dioscorides' *De Materia Medica*, an encyclopedia of herbs and other cures. Most importantly, under the tutelage of the clever monk, the equally bright Joan was able to expand on and sharpen her language skills.

It was supposedly around the year 830 that the friendship between 15-year-old Joan and the monk blossomed into romance. Initially, the monk's nagging guilt nibbled at his conscience. Breaking the vow of celibacy was the worst of all monastic violations. Though he had maintained a relatively clean record up to this point, the abbot, if he were to ever find out, would not take it well, to say the least. He had a feeling this would mean more than just exclusion from group prayers and activities. This could mean permanent banishment from the order.

At the same time, neither one of them could deny that they had established an inevitable connection. Their feelings deepened, and the pent-up sexual tension between the pair only intensified over time. At the same time, they knew this would never last – it would only be a matter of time before someone caught them in the act.

In the middle of class one day, an idea came hurtling out of left field. For years, Joan had continued to express a vigorous interest in pursuing a formal education, and her academic promise was one the monk had never, and might never, come across again. Now, there was no way Joan could ever be enrolled in Fulda, but "John" certainly could. And thus, the plan was hatched.

It was preposterous indeed, but it was so crazy, it just might work.

Camouflage and the Papacy

"Human behavior flows from three main sources: desire, emotion, and knowledge." – Plato

One dark, cloudless night, Joan stood at the foot of her parents' bed, her heart tightening as she memorized the rhythmic rising and falling of their slumbering bodies. Exhaling deeply, she bade them a silent farewell and scurried out into the quiet streets. Her glistening hands felt strangely empty and her mind was racing with jumbled, hesitant thoughts, but there was no turning back now.

A breathless Joan sprinted towards the clearing behind the Fulda Monastery. Out of nowhere, a pair of arms swung out from the shadows, seizing her by the shoulders. The wide-eyed Joan blinked back at her lover, who had been waiting for her for quite some time. Their hearts flooded with emotion at the sight of each other, but there was no time left to waste.

The taboo twosome went to work immediately. Joan's flowing fair hair was crudely sawed off, her locks falling silently into the dirt around her feet. As she knelt down for the tonsure treatment, she dug up loose patches of soil and buried the incriminating locks in the ground. Finally, the monk handed Joan one of his extra habits, which fortunately did nothing for her figure. The transformation was complete.

The next morning, the monk requested for a meeting with the abbot and his superiors. Before long, a fellow monk approached them to inform them that they had been summoned. With bated breath, Joan and her lover marched through the cloister walk, past the refectory, and into the abbot's station. The head of the Fulda Monastery was Abbot Rabanus Maurus, who would later become the archbishop of Mainz. Maurus was a studious character known for his numerous commentaries on Scripture, and he was a man of unwavering discipline and austerity. This would be a character most difficult to impress.

A medieval depiction of Maurus (far left) presenting his work to Archbishop Otgar of Mainz

Joan and her lover locked eyes for a brief moment, but they faced the belly of the beast head on. The monk introduced his new companion as "John Anglicus," an old friend from his childhood. "John" cleared his throat and deepened the sound of his voice, and relayed the story the conspiring pair had concocted beforehand. "John" explained that he had always felt a calling to spread the word of the Lord, and was ready to devote his life to the order and their sacred mission.

The candidate, or postulant, had mentioned an expertise in more than 3 languages, which was sweet music to the abbot's ears. During this time, the Benedictines were in the process of developing and expanding on new languages, including Spanish, Italian, and French. A master linguist was just who they needed on board. For a few moments, Abbot Maurus regarded the aspiring monk, his steely face void of expression. "John" held his gaze, hiding his fidgeting fingers under the thick sleeves of his cloak. At last, the satisfied abbot shattered the suspense, sending them on their way.

By the end of the week, Joan had taken the vow of obedience. As a new monk, her postulancy, otherwise known as a monastic probationary period, would last a month. This was another 30 days Joan would effortlessly breeze through. Careful not to draw any attention to herself, Joan followed the schedules to a T, and interacted only with her lover, and in time, a handful of other monks. For the first time ever, she was taking part in a real, formal education, and blowing this opportunity was the last thing on her mind.

Just how was Joan able to blend in so seamlessly in a monastery full of men – for years? For one, Joan never had to shed her habit in front of anyone (other than her lover). Back then, in certain parts of the world, the act of bathing was linked to "sexual debauchery." To the religious, it was a way for the devil to enter the exposed soul. While Medieval Europeans began to scrub the dirt and grime off their faces with warm water, wine, or vinegar, bathing was still a luxury reserved for the rich. Most monks were allowed their own basins so they could wash their hands, feet, and neck from time to time. Clergy members were also required to stay clean shaven, so Joan's perpetually smooth face never aroused any unwanted suspicion. And while some of her peers might have noticed her small, slender stature, this, again, was not an uncommon sight. The scrawny "John Anglicus" was raised in a poor family, and therefore, they concluded that it must have been years of malnutrition that stunted his growth.

Ultimately, it was this very advantage that would nearly undo Joan. Townspeople could no longer smell the fetid stench wafting out of the open sewers. The open ditches, which were overflowing with garbage, excrement, and animal corpses, trickled into rivers and lakes, contaminating the only clean water supply. The fleas and rodents lurking in every nook and cranny only brought another host of diseases. Coupled with the lack of personal hygiene at the time, common Europe was a breeding ground for disease.

In time, both Joan and her lover had fallen ill. They ground up different herbs and slathered the thick pastes onto their skin. They tried blood-letting, an ancient medical procedure that involved drawing out the "excess blood" in one's system with leeches or incisions. They consulted astrological medical charts and munched on raw roots. They seemed to try every cure in the book, but their terrible fevers only deteriorated. As the Catholic Church preached that illnesses were God's punishment for sinful behavior, the morality behind the lovebirds' double lives must have crossed their minds.

The Fulda monks began to take notice of "John's" waxy complexion. "He" would claim to be fine, brushing them off repeatedly, but one of the worried superiors eventually called for one of the monastery physicians to check up on him. Joan and her lover found ways to stall, but they needed a new plan, and fast. If Joan landed herself with a handsy physician who discovered certain features of her anatomy, that would be the end of things for both of them.

With deep apologies, Joan dismissed the physician once more and requested for him to come back tomorrow morning instead. That night, while the other monks snoozed in their cells, Joan and her lover crept out of bed, tiptoed through the cloister walk, and out the back door. The fleeing lovers climbed onto a stallion from the monastery stable and rode into the night, heading for the Greek city of Athens.

Tragically, some say the tale of these 2 lovers stops here. After a few weeks, Joan would eventually make a full recovery, but the Benedictine monk would succumb to his illness and pass on shortly after. Others say that the young lovers eventually drifted apart and went their separate ways, with her ex-lover heading east in pursuit of a different course of study.

Either way, the sources claimed that Joan, now in her 20s, settled in Athens and continued her life as an English priest, Father John Anglicus. Her heart ached for the partner she had lost, and at times, the intimidated Joan felt like a fish out of water, but she would not let herself lose focus. Armed with years of experience and an education that surpassed the majority of her peers, she began to grow comfortable in John's skin. The sky was the limit. John Anglicus began to give public lectures on the streets, his rapidly growing audience lured by his easy eloquence. Many began to remember this name.

John Anglicus would soon create a solid reputation around town as an advocate for the Latin stance on the *filioque* controversy. The *filioque* debate was one that had been sparked about 1 or 2 centuries earlier when the Nicene Creed was altered. The line, which had previously read, "I believe...in the Holy Ghost, which comes from the Father," had been updated to: "...the Holy Ghost, which comes from the Father *and Son*." As frivolous as this slight addition might seem, it caused a massive row that eventually led to the split of the Roman Catholic and Eastern Orthodox Churches in the year 1054.

In the year 847, 32-year-old Joan packed up her belongings and hitched a ride to the city of Rome. Joan found herself a cheap, but cozy room for rent, and began to look for a teaching job. For a few months, she taught science in all-male schools and worked part-time as a notary at the *curia* (the public council) to pay the bills. She continued to speak openly on numerous subjects, including the defense of image worship, another trending topic of the time. In a matter of months, all the leaders of the Catholic Church in the Vatican knew the name of Father John Anglicus.

Joan was later approached by senior church members, who invited the priest to work in the Vatican. She was awarded even more students, and resumed with the teachings of several sciences and foreign languages, including Greek. When she was not in the classroom, she was in the *scriptorium*, scribbling away. Gradually, Joan gained the respect of her peers, who often praised the priest for "his" exceptional language abilities, exemplary conduct, and excellent conversational and orating skills.

In another year or so, Father John Anglicus had become so beloved that he was promoted to cardinal. The rank of cardinal was among the highest honors of the Roman Catholic Church.

Cardinals, who were the most senior members of the priesthood, acted as a private consultant for the pope himself. Additionally, cardinals were in charge of their own ministries, which included responsibilities such as attending regular meetings, disciplining and doling out punishments to the clergy, and filling vacant posts. An exalted Joan welcomed her new title with open arms.

Around this time, it is said that Joan would take on a new lover. Like the first love of her life, no one seems to know for sure who this new lover was. Some say she had been chased by a chamberlain, an officer in charge of a nobleman's household. Others say she had been seduced by a servant. Most agree this mystery man was another cardinal from a neighboring city.

But one of the most interesting theories about the identity of Joan's lover would come hundreds of years later. A 16th century historian, Onofrio Panvinio, theorized that Joan had been one of Pope John XII's many alleged mistresses, even though the timing of Pope John XII's life came nowhere near matching the earlier legends about Joan. This infamous pope was only 18 when he rose to the papal throne in the year 955. Those that served under the young pope called him reckless and immature. He would be dogged by a litany of charges throughout his 9 year reign, including being accused of gambling, corruption, murder, mutilation, invoking demons, and "turning the papal palace into a whorehouse."

Pope John XII

Regardless of the frisky pope's history, which included accusations of engaging in adultery with 2 widows, a niece, and making a move on his father's girlfriend, Joan had apparently fallen under the spell of the ladies' man. It was said that she had stayed faithful to her man for close to

20 years, and remained so, even when he died at 27 in the middle of intercourse with a local prostitute. Historians still argue about the cause of the pope's death. Some insist that he died of a hemorrhage and stroke complications, while others agree that he was murdered, with some speculating a jealous husband or boyfriend. According to Panvinio, Joan believed her lover had been murdered by bitter church rivals, and vowed to avenge his death. It was with the aid of the murdered pope's allies that Joan was able to infiltrate the Vatican.

A Pope, A Baby, and an Unforgettable Procession

"Justice is the constant and perpetual wish to render everyone his due." – Emperor Justinian I, Ruler of the Byzantine Empire

On July 17, 855, the gloomy streets of Rome mourned the passing of Pope Leo IV. Joan, backed by cardinals from other cities, took on the papal duties temporarily. Following a careful deliberation by the papal conclave over the next couple of weeks, the College of Cardinals had come to a decision. Joan was selected as the new pope, the almighty head of the Catholic Church. To the world, she was Pope John VIII.

A depiction of Pope Leo IV

A 19th century depiction of Pope John VIII

If Joan were to travel back in time and tell herself about the greatness she would achieve by the age of 40, never in a million years would the young Joan have believed it.

In 9th century Europe, the pope was at the peak of the Catholic pyramid, hailed as the "ultimate representative" of God on earth. God's messengers were to be treated like royalty, and their high status granted them extensive privileges. They were revered by the public, as almost everyone was deeply religious. They held so much influence that they practically held more power than the ruler in certain territories.

Papal approval ratings greatly overshadowed the ratings of monarchs and emperors, as the pope was selected by learned judges, whereas the latter inherited their thrones through their bloodlines. This often resulted in a power struggle between the pope and the ruler. One of the main, long-lasting feuds concerned their failure to reach an agreement on church organization. Some kings and emperors asserted that they should have had the power to select the bishops for their cities, but the church refused them that right.

   The papal lifestyle was nothing like the taxing everyday toils and drudgery of a run-of-the-mill monk. Joan, or Pope John VIII, moved into the princely Lateran Palace on the Caelian Hill, in southeast Rome. The elegant estate was home to a massive *triclinium*, which served as the formal state banqueting hall, its walls and ceilings decorated with colorful mosaics. Next to the palace was the Archbasilica of St. John Lateran, Rome's principal cathedral. Tucked away inside the cathedral was the cloister courtyard, a square of lush, green land guarded by spiral columns studded with more breathtaking mosaics.

Lateran Square with the palace in the background

A 17th century engraving of the Lateran Palace

Joan no longer had to wear those wretched, rag-like cloaks. As the pope, she now wore distinctive papal liturgical vestments, which included a crisp, floor-length tunic, a papal tiara, and silk stockings. Alas, it wasn't just all glitz and glamor. The pope needed to be a fast learner, as they were given a whole new world of responsibilities. Everyone turned to the pope. They sought him out not just for guidance on prayer or clarifications on holy texts, but depended on the papal authority to steer them towards the path of righteousness.

The pope alone had the power to decide what the Church would preach, and had the say to adjust or to eliminate antiquated doctrines and start from scratch if they so wished. This could be done through the issuing of letters, known as "papal bulls," which were also used to better explain doctrines, or outline updated church policies. Last, but not least, the pope, and the pope alone held the key to excommunication. This meant they had the right to call out anyone for heresy or any act of impertinence against the church, and expel them from the community for good. Few would dare get on the pope's bad side, as it was widely believed that excommunication automatically rendered their ticket to heaven void.

As legend would have it, Joan's papal reign was cursed with trouble from the beginning. She found herself smack dab in the middle of what historians now describe as "a period of confusion." The Beneventian War, a product of Frankish King and Holy Roman Emperor Charlemagne, had come to a close by the middle of the 8th century, but cities all over Europe were still scrambling to pick up the pieces. First, there were the Saracen raids. "Saracen" was a term coined by early Christian writers, which referred to Muslim Arab defectors from the once

Roman province of Arabia. Starting around 846, Saracen raiders and plunderers descended upon the outskirts of southern Italy. For years, Saracen mobs destroyed basilicas, government buildings, and other priceless Roman treasures. Whatever art the attackers could get their hands on became nothing but ashes. Homes were looted clean and set ablaze. Women were raped, and civilians left and right brutally slain. In 849, a Saracen group succeeded in taking over the port city of Ostia. 3 years later, another Saracen stronghold was erected in Bari, another port city. Here, the Saracens established a political territory claimed by the Islamic monarch, otherwise known as an emirate, was founded. A year later, Italy was struck with another blow when a palace revolt in the city of Salerno that saw Prince Sico II hurled off his throne.

Mother Nature wasn't doing Italy any favors, either. Hundreds upon hundreds of homes were built along the banks of the Tiber River, a wide babbling body of water that stretches across the city of Rome. Apart from the lack of secure walls or dams around the banks, the irregular width of the river bed made the city prone to bouts of intense flooding during rainy seasons. Flooding was so frequent that this kicked off the traditional usage of hydrometers, which were calibrated systems used to measure flood levels. Each time the record was broken, a new plaque would be erected somewhere in the city to memorialize the event.

Around the same time, Roman fields were invaded by swarms of locusts. These tropical grasshoppers spread across the fields in droves, causing severe damage to crops and plantation. In turn, the increasing deficiency of edible crops led to famine, and the food shortage incited even more panic. It had become such a problem that authorities began to offer rewards to anyone who could present a certain number of locust corpses.

The details behind Joan's achievements as pope have always been skimped on in every account of her story. The biographies of Pope John VIII, however, may shed more insight into the subject. At the beginning of his papacy, he issued a ban against forming alliances with any Saracens. He would later travel to 5 Italian cities and provinces to try to settle disputes with Muslim raiders. The pope would also be credited with crowning Louis II, the King of France, as well as anointing 2 Holy Roman emperors.

Throughout Joan's reign as pope, she carried on a secret relationship with her new lover, a cardinal. Other historians claim that her first amour, the Benedictine monk, had returned from the east and rekindled the flames of their romance. Whether it was during a rollicking rendezvous with the cardinal, or a fiery fling with the monk, eventually Joan became pregnant.

On one fateful day about 9 months later, the pope was asked to perform an excommunication on the lethal locusts. Excommunication with locusts, snakes, and other pesky creatures was the medieval version of pest control. This involved hosing down fields and vegetation with holy water, which seemed effective, as these pests would eventually vacate the fields. Some may find this absurd, as insects have and never will take part in religious, or any human rites, but medieval Europeans believed these swarms were an act of God or Satan. Either way, religious intervention would be required to drive them out forever.

At the time, Joan found that if she just slouched a little, her perfect beach ball belly disappeared behind her loose papal robes. Still, in a time before prenatal vitamins or electric heating pads, Joan must have been fighting through some serious pain. This could have only been made worse by the sweltering, sticky heat of the summer and the added weight of the chunky papal tiara.

Nonetheless, Joan braved the immense discomfort, tightening her grip around her grand triple barred cross as her portable throne proceeded through the dirt streets of Via Sacra ("The Sacred Way"). She had already come this far. Just 500 more feet or so, and she would be home free. Behind her, an oblivious line of assistant ministers, including the cardinal, followed in tow. They recited prayers with her, each bearing their own wooden croziers.

And then it happened. As the throne reached the narrow lane between St. Clement's Basilica and the Clement Colosseum, she started to feel sick. The procession was instantly ceased, and one thing led to another. The horses and the wheels of the throne screeched to a halt. Joan staggered out of the *sede gestiatora* and tripped over her own feet. The cross slipped out of her hands, clattering onto the ground. The crowd cried out in shock, many throwing out their arms instinctively. Around Joan, the assistant ministers hastened to her aid at once. They attempted to help her off the ground, but Joan batted them away with flailing arms.

The burning cramping sensations were becoming more frequent, and the muscles around her uterus began constricting. Her skin was red-hot to the touch. Sweat was oozing out of every pore in her body. There was no denying it, or delaying it: Joan was going into labor. The ministers and crowds were frozen in silence as they watched the scene unfold. Joan had never arranged for any midwives, nor did she have any oils or pungent poultices to somewhat ease the pain. This was a task no mother would want for themselves – Joan had to deliver the baby herself. She leaned back, her legs splayed apart. In a matter of minutes, the baby began to crown. The crowds went ballistic. Many gasped, slapping their hands onto the sides of their slacked jaws. Some lunged forth with their fists raised, only to be held back by those around them. Others were stooping over in a circle, fanning the unconscious.

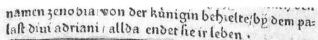

A woodcut engraving depicting the pope giving birth

Most who have told Joan's story agree that it was ultimately her pride that had led to her fall from grace. She must have known that she might give birth at any minute, and yet she insisted upon resuming with the procession.

As to what happened after the birth of the baby, the stories of Pope Joan's end vary quite a bit. Some say Joan died from labor complications, slowly bleeding out to the jeers of the angry crowd. Another account ends with the riotous crowd breaking through and tackling both Joan and the child, viciously tearing off the limbs of the devil pope and her spawn. Others say Joan and her child were tethered to the legs of horses and dragged through the streets of Rome as a mob flung stones and boulders at them. A few claim that authorities arrested Joan and separated her from her child, and later hanged her in the city square.

For example, the medieval chronicle *Chronicon Pontificum et Imperatorum*, authored by

Martin of Opava, didn't relay to readers the cause of death but implied that the pope died during the procession: "John Anglicus, born at Mainz, was Pope for two years, seven months and four days, and died in Rome, after which there was a vacancy in the Papacy of one month. It is claimed that this John was a woman, who as a girl had been led to Athens dressed in the clothes of a man by a certain lover of hers. There she became proficient in a diversity of branches of knowledge, until she had no equal, and, afterward in Rome, she taught the liberal arts and had great masters among her students and audience. A high opinion of her life and learning arose in the city; and she was chosen for Pope. While Pope, however, she became pregnant by her companion. Through ignorance of the exact time when the birth was expected, she was delivered of a child while in procession from St. Peter's to the Lateran, in a lane once named Via Sacra (the sacred way) but now known as the 'shunned street' between the Colosseum and St Clement's church. After her death, it is said she was buried in that same place. The Lord Pope always turns aside from the street, and it is believed by many that this is done because of abhorrence of the event. Nor is she placed on the list of the Holy Pontiffs, both because of her female sex and on account of the foulness of the matter."

Similarly, Bartolomeo Platina, who wrote *Vitæ Pontificum Platinæ historici liber de vita Christi ac omnium pontificum qui hactenus ducenti fuere et XX* in the late 15th century, relied on Martin of Opava as a source when writing a historical account for Pope Sixtus IV: "Pope John VIII: John, of English extraction, was born at Mentz (Mainz) and is said to have arrived at popedom by evil art; for disguising herself like a man, whereas she was a woman, she went when young with her paramour, a learned man, to Athens, and made such progress in learning under the professors there that, coming to Rome, she met with few that could equal, much less go beyond her, even in the knowledge of the scriptures; and by her learned and ingenious readings and disputations, she acquired so great respect and authority that upon the death of Pope Leo IV (as Martin says) by common consent she was chosen pope in his room. As she was going to the Lateran Church between the Colossean Theatre (so called from Nero's Colossus) and St. Clement's her travail came upon her, and she died upon the place, having sat two years, one month, and four days, and was buried there without any pomp. This story is vulgarly told, but by very uncertain and obscure authors, and therefore I have related it barely and in short, lest I should seem obstinate and pertinacious if I had admitted what is so generally talked. I had better mistake with the rest of the world, though it be certain, that what I have related may be thought not altogether incredible."

On the other hand, one historian contends that the cardinals and other associates swooped in and rescued Joan and her child from the chaos in the nick of time. She was later sent away to a secluded convent to raise her child, where they lived out the rest of their lives in peace. Her child would supposedly grow up to become the Bishop of Ostia.

Either way, after the birth of the child, the Italian scholar Petrarch wrote about the waves of terror that crashed over Europe, reminiscent of the biblical plagues: [I]n Brescia it rained blood for 3 days and 3 nights. In France there appeared marvelous locusts, which had 6 wings and very powerful teeth. They flew miraculously in the air, and all drowned in the British Sea. The golden bodies were rejected by the waves of the sea and corrupted the air, so that a great many people died."

Analyzing the Legend

" [A] female pope, who is not set down in the list of popes, who by an occurrence of wonderful audacity, was made pope – Johanna, a woman, for which reason she does not bear a number to her name..." – Jean de Mailly

Over 1,000 years after the story of Pope Joan allegedly took place, it is nearly impossible to find a modern Italian who does not know the story by heart. The lane of Via Sacra still stands, one that they say is so despised by the Catholic Church that the pope still goes out of his way to avoid the street today. And while most historians are quick to dismiss the story of Pope Joan as nothing more than ancient folklore, there are those who point disbelievers to a mountain of alleged evidence.

To begin with, naysayers question the scattered and extremely varying details over the 500 or so accounts written by historians over the centuries. To this, believers in the legend claim they have an answer. Judging by the antiquated record system of the Early Middle Ages, one could question the veracity of all other accepted stories of the time. This was an era when most people were illiterate and did not even have last names – no one needed them, as most would stay within their villages their entire lives. Thus, only the core of Pope Joan's story would survive.

During an interview conducted in a documentary by ABC, Donna Woolfolk Cross, the author of *Pope Joan*, reminded the audience that most of the historians who had written about Joan were Catholics. These were not just monks, nuns, or former religious leaders, but often "Catholics very highly placed in the papal hierarchy." It would not make sense, at least according to Cross, for these Catholics to fabricate such a story, and such an exaggerated tale at that. Peter Stanford, author of *The She Pope*, backed up this claim, stating, "Among the phalanx of authors who testify unambiguously to her existence are papal servants, several bishops, and some of the most distinguished and respected medieval chroniclers, writers whose accounts are the bedrock of current historical and church orthodoxy about their period."

Better yet, those who believe in the female pope's historicity say there is concrete evidence woven into European art and literature. In the book *Il Decameron*, penned by Giovanni Boccaccio, Pope Joan placed number 51 on the list of famous women. Not too far from the infamous Via Sacra, in the junction between Via Santi Quattro and dei Querceti, lies a small, rusty portico with a tin roof, an ancient shrine devoted to Pope Joan – "The Shrine of Papessa Giovanna." Near this shrine is a faded thousand-year-old painting of a woman and her child, supposedly Joan. About 60% of the color and imagery on the painting is rubbed off, which is a testament to its age.

Believers also point to another clue: the "High Priestess" tarot card. This card, which joined the circulation around the beginning of the 15th century, was once known as the "*La Papessa*" – or in English, "The Popess." The image of the handsome, solemn-faced woman is often said to have been of Pope Joan. Other historians argue that the character featured on the card was actually Maifreda Visconti, who had attempted to declare herself Pope of Milan in the 1300s but was quickly deposed and burnt at the stake.

Tarot cards depicting the Popess

Other clues can allegedly be found in the time-honored cathedrals of Italy. The Siena Cathedral is home to a clustered collection of 170 or so terracotta busts that line the walls, featuring popes throughout the ages. Caesar Baronius, a 16th century ecclesiastical historian, documented that one of those busts had once been female. The bust in question is of none other than Pope Joan, which included the inscription, "*Johanna, De Papa Femina*," or "Joan, the Female Pope." Baronius professed that a Renaissance priest had grown enraged at the sight of it and ordered for its destruction at once. The sculptor did as he was told, but rather than start from scratch, Joan's face was chiseled out and replaced with the face of Pope Zacharias instead.

Another set of suspicious clues lies in St. Peter's Basilica itself, particularly, the 2 marble columns by the *baldacchino*. 8 distinctive crests are engraved into these columns, which were supposedly commissioned by Pope Urban VIII. The artist, Gian Lorenzo Bernini, had been assigned to head the project, and was tasked with designing the coat of arms for the pope. 7 of these crests portray a woman in the stages of labor. The last crest shows the image of a giggling, round-faced baby with a full head of curls. These crests, many believe, pay homage to Joan's painful childbirth.

Peter Sanford's book, which examines the myth, provides more clues. The Welsh priest and medieval chronicler Adam of Usk once wrote about 2 statues of Joan and her child, one which was said to have stood near St. Clement's Basilica, and the other by the Colosseum. The Catholic Church was said to have gotten rid of them. Later, based on the account of a 15th century secretary, a new, grisly statue of Joan in bloody labor stood in its place, supposedly set up by the Catholic Church to frighten and warn the public about the great deception.

Among these lost files, as told by Usk, is an eye-opening medieval document. This file purportedly claims that it was because of Joan that the naturally effeminate Pope Innocent VII had to be patted down several times by suspicious authorities, under instruction to double-check his gender. Another papal document allegedly holds proof of an account that Pope Innocent VIII was once reprimanded for strolling through the cursed street.

Yet another compelling piece of evidence comes from an excerpt in *Colloquia Mensalia,* written by Martin Luther, the legendary figure who helped spearhead the Protestant Reformation. According to Luther, while he was visiting Rome in 1510, he chanced upon a puzzling sight. He wrote, "In Rome, in a public square, there is a stone monument to commemorate the pope who was really a woman and gave birth to a child on that very spot. I have seen the stone myself, and I find it astonishing that the popes permit it to exist."

Luther

There exists one medieval enigma that many say directly correlates with that of Pope Joan – the mystery of the missing pope. If one were to gloss over the compiled list of all the popes that have reigned since the beginning of time, it would be easy to skip the seemingly innocent entry. Between the names of anti-pope Boniface VII and John XV, there was John XX. Modern historians claim that this was the result of a mix up made by 13th century chroniclers, and that this pope never existed. Some put the blame on anti-popes of the time (unofficial popes established by opposing parties who rejected the canonized pope). They had supposedly taken the title for themselves, adding to the confusion.

But again, others began to speculate. A few conspiracy theorists noticed that all this confusion had begun around Joan's time. Anti-papal rebels from the Renaissance had also supported this claim, announcing that the missing pope scandal was nothing more but a distraction to bury the truth about Joan.

Truth-seekers maintain that this was far from the first, nor would it be the last, of the Catholic Church's countless coverups. If one was to take author Donna Cross' word for it, the clergymen of the time would have resorted to extreme measures to "bury all written report [sic] of this embarrassing episode." Hincmar, the Archbishop of Reims, and one who had lived in Joan's time, was said to have admitted to tampering and suppressing toxic or character-damaging information about the Church, under orders from his superiors. The English scholar and mathematician Alcuin had also confessed to shredding a report that contained both allegations and proof to Pope Leo III's alleged corruption and adulterous affairs.

Finally, there was the *sedia stercoraria*. This was the name of the purple marble chair that would be used in papal coronations after Joan's alleged reign. The striking chair had a curved but rigid back, and its seat a gaping keyhole-shaped opening in its center. Rumor has it that cardinals and deacons were made to crawl underneath the chair and stick their hands through the hole during coronations to feel up His Holiness. Once the necessary "items" were detected, the minister would emerge from underneath the seat and declare to the crowd, *"Duos habet et bene pendentes!"* Or, in English, "He has two, and they dangle nicely!" At times, ministers of few words would simply utter, *"habet!"* – "he has them!"

This very chair supposedly still exists today, stowed away from the public eye in the heart of the Vatican museum.

A Myth Debunked?

"In any case, the fact is there was no Pope Joan. She exists only as pure legend, but one that makes for a sexy story." – Patrick Madrid, *Envoy for Christ: 25 Years as a Catholic Apologist*

It appears that the disproving of Joan's existence has been around far longer than many might think. Naysayers have been making themselves heard since as early as the 15th century. Respected scholars such as Platina and Aeneas Silvius were among the first to dissect the messy accounts and write them off as fiction. A century later, other veteran chroniclers confirmed their findings.

Most modern historians today have arrived at the same verdict. As electrifying as the story of Pope Joan is, they believe that is simply all it is – a story. Hundreds of books, articles, essays, and blog posts have since been written to dispel the fiction of what they call the mythical female pope.

One of the most damning proofs to discredit Pope Joan is also arguably the simplest of them all. The muddled details and constantly changing events of her story is the first red flag. Polonus' 1265 excerpt on Joan had been the most detailed of the accounts yet, and the stories that were spun after only grew increasingly more elaborate.

Professor Valerie Hotchkiss, an expert on medieval studies from Southern Methodist University, has alluded to the fact that Polonus had never actually written the section on Pope Joan. Said Hotchkiss, "So he didn't write it, but it was put in very soon after his death, like around 1280 to 1290. And everyone picks it up from Martin Polonus...And they're picking it up from each other, and changing it and embellishing it."

As a direct response to why there has been at least 500 historical accounts, historians have hit back with an answer. Monks and other scribes of the Middle Ages were essentially "medieval copy machines." Translating and copying texts were thankless, tedious jobs, and were ones that kept scribes busy for the better parts of their days – some of them, almost every day. These historians are confident that these accounts had come from scribes who were replicating the false information that had been handed to them, whether they were aware of it or not.

Monsignor Charles Burns, the ex-head of the Vatican secret archives, agreed with Hotchkiss. He explained that medieval people, like those who prolong the legend today, had been taken by the sensational story. Given their lack of entertainment, they were quick to sop up the story, despite the absence of proof or factual evidence. What was more, Burns firmly states that in all the files in the secret archives, records that run 100dozens of miles long, there has never been a single mention of Pope Joan.

Piggybacking on the supposedly erroneous Polonus account, historians have also pointed out the mismatching dates and events. Polonus claimed that Joan, or "Pope John VIII," had come into power right after the death of Pope Leo IV, and would only later be succeeded by Pope Benedict III. However, evidence exists that proves it was Pope Benedict III who was the heir to the papal throne.

To add more spice to the cauldron, there was in fact, an actual Pope John VIII. Only, he was said to have reigned between December of 872 and December of 882, these dates snugly fitting between the reigns of Adrian II and Marinus I. This is seen as yet another strike against Polonus, as the dates in his account clearly do not add up to those in the Joan legend.

Those who believe Joan existed have often questioned the missing 2 months between the official dates of Leo IV and Benedict III's dominions. Those teetering on the fence suggest that this might be proof of Joan's existence. Maybe her story had been aggrandized, but not entirely fictional – could it be that there really was a Pope Joan under a different name, who, rather than 2 years, ruled for 2 months?

As it turns out, historians seemed to have found an explanation for the missing piece of the puzzle. Pope Benedict III had indeed been elected by clergymen and the Romans on July 17, 855, the day of Leo IV's demise. However, the Anti-pope Anastasius Bibliothecarius had been elected by the imperial party, which led to a tense standoff. Benedict III was only officially sanctified and recognized by the public in September of that year. The 1910 Catholic

Encyclopedia discussed this crucial period: "Between Leo IV and Benedict III, where Martinus Polonus places her, she cannot be inserted, because Leo IV died 17 July 855, and immediately after his death Benedict III was elected by the clergy and people of Rome; but, owing to the setting up of an Antipope, in the person of the deposed Cardinal Anastasius, he was not consecrated until 29 September. Coins exist which bear both the image of Benedict III and of Emperor Lothair, who died 28 September 855; therefore Benedict must have been recognized as pope before the last-mentioned date. On 7 October 855, Benedict III issued a charter for the Abbey of Corvey. Hincmar, Archbishop of Reims, informed Nicholas I that a messenger whom he had sent to Leo IV learned on his way of the death of this Pope, and therefore handed his petition to Benedict III, who decided it (Hincmar, ep. xl in P.L., CXXXVI, 85). All these witnesses prove the correctness of the dates given in the lives of Leo IV and Benedict III, and there was no interregnum between these two Popes, so that at this place there is no room for the alleged Popess."

Moreover, the Roman coins that still reside in museums today give the above facts another angle. One particular silver coin depicts the crudely stamped faces of Pope Benedict III on one side, and Emperor Lothair I on the other, with the names of these venerated leaders etched around the edges. Lothair I died on September 29, 855, which historians take to mean that Pope Benedict III had already been in power before the death of the emperor.

There are also documents that contain the handwriting of the actual Pope Benedict III, which can still be found in Roman archives. Among these documents is a charter for the Abbey of Corvey, which was dated October 7, 855. There appears to have been no room for Pope Joan at all – at least not Polonus' version the story, anyway.

This still leaves enduring questions, though. If Pope Joan truly is nothing but a tall tale, how and why did these stories come about in the first place? Yet again, there are different theories. Whereas some believe that Joan's lack of mention between the 9th and 13th centuries had been the result of a Roman Catholic mass coverup conspiracy, most historians claim that Joan had been an imaginary figure devised during the Protestant Reformation to "discredit the papacy." Popes at the time had a bad reputation for shoving their noses into politics and military conflicts, which left a sour taste in the public's mouth. It was a time of turbulent turmoil, especially within the church, one that would have made a conspiracy of this enormity an impossibility.

Between the 13th and 15th centuries, more and more women were beginning to step out of the shadows, such as the rise of the Beguines and Mystics. Women began to demand an identity for themselves, and though unwelcome, they began to penetrate the fields of arts and sciences. One of these famous "Mystics" was Hildegard of Bingen. Hildegard was a learned doctor, a composer of music, a playwright, and even dabbled in politics. One theory suggests that the Catholic Church, who feared that these women would one day overpower them, engineered the story of Joan to scare these women into submission.

A medieval depiction of Hildegard of Bingen

Saint Robert Bellarmine had another idea. Bellarmine proposed that the story had been fabricated in Constantinople before making its way to Rome. In the Early Middle Ages, the city of Rome was on the verge of collapsing, and apparently the king of Constantinople wanted to take advantage of Rome's seeming decline because he wanted control of the church.

Bellarmine

Other historians claim that the story of Pope Joan was simply a rumor that had spiraled wildly out of control, which were allegedly based on reports of Pope John VIII's "effeminate weakness."

Yet another glaring piece of evidence provided by critics is the fact that virtually none of the Roman Catholic Church's enemies in the 9th century ever once hinted at a female pope. In the year 858, Photius I became the Patriarch of Constantinople, and he supposedly displayed such animosity over the Catholic Church that he was formally deposed by Pope Nicholas I 5 years later. It would've been of immense value to cite the stupendous shame a female pope would have brought upon the Church, but there has never been a single mention of the scandal in the extensive volumes of Photius I's works. An excerpt that can actually be retrieved from one of his books only adds another layer of believability to these critics' claims: "Leo and Benedict, successively great priests of the Roman Church."

In the year 1570, the Roman Catholic Church formally denounced the legend, but to this very day, a fraction of the population continues to believe in the existence of Pope Joan. The jaded shrug this off as nothing more than anti-Catholic propaganda, and to a few, it is myth spewed by those propagating a "feminist agenda." But of course, everyone loves a conspiracy theory, and while modern myth busters might say that they have more than debunked this legend, the courageous tale of the plucky Pope Joan is a story that will likely be passed on for centuries to come.

Online Resources

Other books about Catholic history by Charles River Editors

Other books about medieval history by Charles River Editors

Other books about Pope Joan on Amazon

Bibliography

1. Editors, Biography.Com. "Pope Joan." *Biography*. A&E Television Networks, LLC, 6 May 2015. Web. 9 Jan. 2017. <http://www.biography.com/people/pope-joan-279083>.

2. Scrivener, Patrick. "Pope Joan." *Reformation.Org*. Patrick Scrivener, n.d. Web. 9 Jan. 2017. <http://www.reformation.org/pope-joan.html>.

3. "Pope Joan: The Female Pope whose Real Gender was Revealed after she Gave Birth in a Procession." *Ancient Origins*. Stella Novus, LLC, 28 May 2015. Web. 9 Jan. 2017. <http://www.ancient-origins.net/history-famous-people/pope-joan-female-pope-whose-real-gender-was-revealed-after-she-gave-birth-020365>.

4. Knight, Kevin. "Popess Joan." *The Catholic Encylopedia*. Robert Appleton Co., 16 Nov. 2016. Web. 9 Jan. 2017. <http://www.newadvent.org/cathen/08407a.htm>.

5. Editors, BeliefNet. "Did a Female Pope Exist?" *BeliefNet*. BeliefNet, Inc., May 2001. Web. 9 Jan. 2017. <http://www.beliefnet.com/faiths/catholic/2001/05/did-a-female-pope-exist.aspx?p=2>.

6. New, Maria I., M.D. "Pope Joan: A Recognizable Syndrome." *National Center for Biotechnology Information*. US National Library of Medicine, n.d. Web. 9 Jan. 2017. <https://www.ncbi.nlm.nih.gov/pmc/articles/PMC2376633/pdf/tacca00084-0162.pdf>.

7. Pardoe, Rosemary, and Darroll Pardoe. "The Female Pope: The Mystery of Pope Joan." *THE FEMALE POPE: THE MYSTERY OF POPE JOAN*. Global Net Co., 1988. Web. 9 Jan. 2017. <http://www.users.globalnet.co.uk/~pardos/PopeJoan1.html>.

8. Stanford, Peter. "Mystery of the pregnant pope: New film reopens one of the Vatican's

most enduring wounds." *Daily Mail*. Associated Newspapers, Ltd., 22 June 2010. Web. 9 Jan. 2017. <http://www.dailymail.co.uk/news/article-1288501/Mystery-pregnant-pope-New-film-reopens-Vaticans-enduring-wounds.html>.

9. Cellenia, Miss. "The Legend of Pope Joan." *Mental Floss*. Mental Floss, Inc., 15 Sept. 2015. Web. 9 Jan. 2017. <http://mentalfloss.com/article/68612/legend-pope-joan>.

10. Editors, Internut. "The Legend of Pope Joan." *The Internut*. Antisocial Media, Inc., Oct. 2015. Web. 9 Jan. 2017. <http://theinternut.net/popejoan.html>.

11. Editors, ABC News. "Looking for Pope Joan." *ABC News*. Walt Disney Co., 29 Dec. 2005. Web. 9 Jan. 2017. <http://abcnews.go.com/Primetime/pope-joan/story?id=1453197>.

12. Editors, Stylist. "The top 50 most empowering feminist quotes of all time." *Stylist*. Stylist, Inc., 22 Sept. 2015. Web. 9 Jan. 2017. <http://www.stylist.co.uk/life/the-top-50-most-empowering-feminist-quotes-of-all-time-women-suffragette-feminism-angelina-jolie-emma-watson#>.

13. Khan, Ejaz. "10 Most Expensive Accidents in History." *WondersList*. WordPress, n.d. Web. 9 Jan. 2017. <http://www.wonderslist.com/10-expensive-accidents-history/>.

14. Lewis, Dan. "Richard Parker." *Now I Know*. Amazon Services LLC Program, 12 June 2012. Web. 9 Jan. 2017. <http://nowiknow.com/richard-parker/>.

15. Grey, Orrin. "DOUBLE LIVES: 6 INFAMOUS REAL-LIFE SECRET IDENTITIES." *The Lineup*. Open Road Integrated Media, n.d. Web. 9 Jan. 2017. <http://www.the-line-up.com/double-lives-6-infamous-real-life-secret-identities/>.

16. Wadler, Joyce. "The True Story of M. Butterfly; The Spy Who Fell in Love With a Shadow." *The New York Times*. The New York Times Company, 15 Aug. 1993. Web. 10 Jan. 2017. <http://www.nytimes.com/1993/08/15/magazine/the-true-story-of-m-butterfly-the-spy-who-fell-in-love-with-a-shadow.html?pagewanted=all>.

17. Manson, Mark. "A BRIEF HISTORY OF MALE/FEMALE RELATIONS." *Mark Manson*. Infinity Squared Media, LLC, 23 Jan. 2014. Web. 10 Jan. 2017. <https://markmanson.net/male-female-relations>.

18. " Women In Patriarchal Societies." *World History Center*. History World International, 1992. Web. 10 Jan. 2017. <http://history-world.org/Civilization,%20women_in_patriarchal_societies.htm>.

19. "The History of Patriarchy." *Women's Resource Center*. Regents of the University of

Colorado, 13 Feb. 2015. Web. 10 Jan. 2017.
<http://www.colorado.edu/wrc/2015/02/13/history-patriarchy>.

20. Editors, Travel China Guide. "Empress Wu Zetian of Tang Dynasty." *Travel China Guide*. Travel China Guide, Ltd., n.d. Web. 10 Jan. 2017.
<https://www.travelchinaguide.com/intro/history/tang/emperor_wuzetian.htm>.

21. Richey, Jeffrey. "Gender and Sexuality." *Patheos Library*. Patheos, Inc., n.d. Web. 10 Jan. 2017. <http://www.patheos.com/Library/Confucianism/Ethics-Morality-Community/Gender-and-Sexuality>.

22. "Confucianism and Gender." *Japan Sociology*. WordPress, 28 Nov. 2011. Web. 10 Jan. 2017. <https://japansociology.com/2011/11/28/confucianism-and-gender/>.

23. Demaria, Meghan. "11 Badass Women In History Who Pretended To Be Men Because Gender Equality Back Then Was More Myth Than Reality." *Bustle Media*. BG Media, Inc., 25 Sept. 2015. Web. 10 Jan. 2017. <https://www.bustle.com/articles/112732-11-badass-women-in-history-who-pretended-to-be-men-because-gender-equality-back-then-was>.

24. Frater, Jamie. "Top 10 Men Who Were Really Women." *Listverse*. Listverse, Ltd., 4 Sept. 2008. Web. 10 Jan. 2017. <http://listverse.com/2008/09/04/top-10-men-who-were-really-women/>.

25. Scribe, The. "The Real Story of Mulan." *The Ancient Standard*. WordPress, 17 June 2011. Web. 10 Jan. 2017. <http://ancientstandard.com/2011/06/17/the-real-story-of-mulan/>.

26. Walker, Jim. "Women's Inferior Status." *No Beliefs*. Jim Walker, 2006. Web. 10 Jan. 2017. <http://www.nobeliefs.com/DarkBible/darkbible7.htm>.

27. Bovey, Alixe. "The Middle Ages." *British Library*. British Library Board, 2014. Web. 10 Jan. 2017. <https://www.bl.uk/the-middle-ages/articles/women-in-medieval-society>.

28. Caster, Yvette. "History period – a look at menstruation through the ages in 15 fascinating facts." *Metro*. Associated Newspapers, Ltd., 20 May 2015. Web. 10 Jan. 2017. <http://metro.co.uk/2015/05/20/history-period-a-look-at-menstruation-through-the-ages-in-15-fascinating-facts-5204085/>.

29. Wijngaards, John. "Women were considered Inferior Creatures." *Women Can Be Priests*. Wijngaards Institute for Catholic Research, n.d. Web. 10 Jan. 2017. <http://www.womenpriests.org/traditio/inferior.asp>.

30. Oliver, Mark. "10 Truly Disgusting Facts About Ancient Roman Life." *Listverse*. Listverse, Ltd., 23 Aug. 2016. Web. 11 Jan. 2017. <http://listverse.com/2016/08/23/10-truly-disgusting-facts-about-roman-life/>.

31. Staff, History.Com. "Did gladiators always fight to the death?" *History Channel*. A&E Television Networks, LLC, 2 Jan. 2013. Web. 11 Jan. 2017. <http://www.history.com/news/ask-history/did-gladiators-always-fight-to-the-death>.

32. "Leviticus 15:19-33." *Bible Study Tools*. Jupiter Images Corporation, 2013. Web. 11 Jan. 2017. <http://www.biblestudytools.com/nlt/leviticus/passage/?q=leviticus 15:19-33>.

33. Breau, Amy. "Why Did Cleopatra Wear Makeup?" *Moment of Science*. Indiana Public Media, 31 Aug. 2012. Web. 11 Jan. 2017. <http://indianapublicmedia.org/amomentofscience/cleopatra-wear-makeup/>.

34. Editors, LordsandLadies.Org. "Daily Life for Peasant Women in the Middle Ages." *Lords and Ladies.Org*. Siteseen, Ltd., Mar. 2015. Web. 11 Jan. 2017. <http://www.lordsandladies.org/daily-life-peasant-women-middle-ages.htm>.

35. Newman, Simon. "Children in the Middle Ages." *The Finer Times*. The Finer Times, Ltd., 19 Oct. 2015. Web. 11 Jan. 2017. <http://www.thefinertimes.com/Middle-Ages/children-in-the-middle-ages.html>.

36. Editors, LordsandLadies.Org. "Middle Ages Food Preservation." *Lords and Ladies.Org*. Siteseen, Ltd., Mar. 2015. Web. 11 Jan. 2017. <http://www.lordsandladies.org/middle-ages-food-preservation.htm>.

37. Editors, J. Paul Getty Museum. "The Medieval Scriptorium." *The J. Paul Getty Museum*. The J. Paul Getty Trust, 24 Nov. 2009. Web. 11 Jan. 2017. <http://www.getty.edu/art/exhibitions/scriptorium/>.

38. Editors, LordsandLadies.Org. "Daily Life of a Monk in the Middle Ages." *Lords and Ladies.Org*. Siteseen, Ltd., Mar. 2015. Web. 11 Jan. 2017. <http://www.lordsandladies.org/daily-life-monk-middle-ages.htm>.

39. Carr, K. E. "What is Tonsure?" *Quatr.Us*. Karen Carr, Portland State University, 7 Jan. 2017. Web. 11 Jan. 2017. <http://quatr.us/religion/christians/tonsure.htm>.

40. Editors, Medievalists.Net. "Sex in the Middle Ages." *Medievalists.Net*. WordPress, 14 Feb. 2013. Web. 11 Jan. 2017. <http://www.medievalists.net/2013/02/sex-in-the-middle-ages/>.

41. Editors, History Undressed. "The rooms in a monastery and their symbolic

meaning." *History Undressed*. Blogspot, 14 July 2008. Web. 11 Jan. 2017.
<http://www.historyundressed.com/2008/07/history-of-hygiene-bathing-teeth.html>.

42. Castelow, Ellen. "Disease in Medieval England." *Historic UK*. Historic UK, Ltd., 2017.
Web. 11 Jan. 2017. <http://www.historic-uk.com/HistoryUK/HistoryofEngland/Disease-
in-Medieval-England/>.

43. Trueman, C. N. "Medicine in the Middle Ages." *The History Learning Site*. The History
Learning Site, Ltd., 17 Mar. 2015. Web. 12 Jan. 2017.
<http://www.historylearningsite.co.uk/a-history-of-medicine/medicine-in-the-middle-
ages/>.

44. Ryrie, Charles. "Question: "What is the filioque clause / filioque controversy?"." *Got
Questions.Org*. Got Questions Ministries, 2015. Web. 12 Jan. 2017.
<https://www.gotquestions.org/filioque-clause-controversy.html>.

45. Knight, Kevin. "Cardinal." *The Catholic Encylopedia*. Robert Appleton Co., 2012. Web.
12 Jan. 2017. <http://www.newadvent.org/cathen/03333b.htm>.

46. Melina, Remy. "7 Quite Unholy Pope Scandals." *Live Science*. Purch, Inc., 17 Sept. 2010.
Web. 12 Jan. 2017. <http://www.livescience.com/8606-7-unholy-pope-scandals.html>.

47. Editors, The Papal Visit. "What is a Cardinal and what is his role?" *The Papal Visit*.
Maryvale Institute, 2014. Web. 12 Jan. 2017. <http://www.thepapalvisit.org.uk/The-
Catholic-Faith/FAQ-on-Faith/1-10/What-is-a-Cardinal-and-what-is-his-role>.

48. Pope, Charles. "What is a Cardinal? The Role of the College of Cardinals in History and
Today." *Community in Mission*. ARCHDIOCESE of WASHINGTON, 1 Mar. 2013.
Web. 12 Jan. 2017. <http://blog.adw.org/2013/03/what-is-a-cardinal-the-role-of-the-
college-of-cardinals-in-history-and-today/>.

49. Warren, Ann K., PhD. "FIVE RELIGIOUS OPTIONS FOR MEDIEVAL
WOMEN." *Christian History Institute*. Christian History Institute, 1991. Web. 12 Jan.
2017. <https://www.christianhistoryinstitute.org/magazine/article/five-religious-options-
for-medieval-women/>.

50. Editors, Medieval Chronicles. "Medieval Pope." *Medieval Chronicles*. Medieval
Chronicles, Inc., 2016. Web. 12 Jan. 2017.
<http://www.medievalchronicles.com/medieval-people/medieval-clergy/medieval-pope-
2/#What_were_a_medieval_popes_duties>.

51. Editors, Medievalists.Net. "20 Great Medieval Quotes." *Medievalists.Net*. WordPress, 17
Aug. 2014. Web. 12 Jan. 2017. <http://www.medievalists.net/2014/08/20-great-

medieval-quotes/>.

52. G, Lauren. "Popes vs. Kings." *The Middle Ages*. Weebly, 2015. Web. 12 Jan. 2017.
    <http://laurengnicoleg.weebly.com/popes-vs-kings.html>.

53. Editors, A View on Cities. "St. John Lateran." *A View on Cities*. A View on Cities, 2017.
    Web. 12 Jan. 2017. <http://www.aviewoncities.com/rome/sangiovanniinlaterano.htm>.

54. "The Muslim Sack of Rome and St Peter's in 846 AD." *Roman Christendom*. Blogspot,
    16 Sept. 2007. Web. 12 Jan. 2017. <http://romanchristendom.blogspot.tw/2007/09/rome-
    was-sacked-by-muslims-in-846-ad.html>.

55. Editors, Virtual Roma. "The Floods Of The River Tiber." *Virtual Roma*. Virtual Roma,
    Ltd., 2013. Web. 12 Jan. 2017. <http://roma.andreapollett.com/S1/roma-c4.htm>.

56. Gilbert, Rosalie. "Medieval Births and Birthing." *Rosalie's Medieval Woman*. Rosalie
    Gilbert, 2015. Web. 12 Jan. 2017. <http://rosaliegilbert.com/births.html>.

57. Editors, Roman Catholicism UK. "THE SHE-POPE." *Roman Catholicism UK*. N.p.,
    2011. Web. 12 Jan. 2017. <http://www.romancatholicism.co.uk/shepope.html>.

58. Smith, Jen. "The legend of Pope Joan and a faded painting." *Med Meanderings*. Jen
    Smith, 8 Sept. 2014. Web. 12 Jan. 2017. <http://medmeanderings.com/history/the-
    legend-of-pope-joan-and-a-faded-painting/>.

59. Editors, Europe a la Carte. "When in Rome: The Legend of Papessa Giovanna (Pope
    Joan)." *Europe a la Carte*. WordPress, 2 Nov. 2010. Web. 12 Jan. 2017.
    <http://www.europealacarte.co.uk/blog/2010/02/11/when-in-rome-the-legend-of-papessa-
    giovanna-pope-joan/>.

60. Madrid, Patrick. "A Primer on the Persistent Myth of "Pope Joan"." *Patrick Madrid*.
    Blogspot, 22 June 2010. Web. 12 Jan. 2017.
    <http://patrickmadrid.blogspot.tw/2009/02/primer-on-persistent-myth-of-pope-
    joan.html>.

61. Editors, Encyclopedia Britannica. "John XX." *Encyclopedia Britannica*. Encyclopedia
    Britannica, Inc., 20 July 1998. Web. 12 Jan. 2017.
    <https://global.britannica.com/topic/John-XX>.

62. Matthew. "QUESTION: WERE THERE WOMEN POPES?" *QUIDQUID EST,
    EST!* WordPress, 31 July 2012. Web. 12 Jan. 2017.
    <https://quidquidestest.wordpress.com/2012/07/31/question-were-there-women-popes/>.

63. Editors, Catholic Straight Answers. "Is there any truth about the legend of "Pope Joan?"." *Catholic Straight Answers*. Catholic Straight Answers, 2017. Web. 12 Jan. 2017. <http://catholicstraightanswers.com/is-there-any-truth-about-the-legend-of-pope-joan/>.

64. Madrid, Patrick. *Envoy for Christ: 25 Years as a Catholic Apologist*. N.p.: Servant , 2012. Print.

65. Lockwood, Jeffrey A. *Locust: The Devastating Rise and Mysterious Disappearance of the Insect that Shaped the American Frontier*. N.p.: Basic , 2005. Print.

66. Bondeson, Jane. *The Feejee Mermaid and Other Essays in Natural and Unnatural History*. N p : Cornell U Press, 2014. Print.

67. Watkins, John, and Carole Levin. *Shakespeare's Foreign Worlds: National and Transnational Identities in the Elizabethan Age*. N.p.: Cornell U Press, 2012. Print.

68. Sawyer, Diane. "Looking for Pope Joan." *ABC News Specials*. American Broadcasting Company. 18 Sept. 2006. Television.

Free Books by Charles River Editors

We have brand new titles available for free most days of the week. To see which of our titles are currently free, click on this link.

Discounted Books by Charles River Editors

We have titles at a discount price of just 99 cents everyday. To see which of our titles are currently 99 cents, click on this link.